DISCARD

eXtreme Games

Summer Action Sports

Jim Brush

SEA-TO-SEA
Mankato Collingwood London

This edition first published in 2013 by
Sea-to-Sea Publications
Distributed by Black Rabbit Books
P.O. Box 3263, Mankato, Minnesota 56002

Printed in the United States of America,
North Mankato, MN

9 8 7 6 5 4 3 2

Published by arrangement with the Watts Publishing Group Ltd, London.

A CIP catalog record is available from the Library of Congress.

ISBN: 978-1-59771-407-5

Series Editor: Adrian Cole
Art Director: Jonathan Hair
Design: Graham Rich Design
Picture Research: Diana Morris

Acknowledgements:

Robyn Beck/AFP/Getty Images: 27. Bo Bridges/Getty Images: 14, 37. Chris Carbon/AP/PAI: 23. Jacque Chong Pictures: 42. Stanley Chou/Getty Images: 43. Tony Donaldson/Topfoto: 7. Stephen Dunn/Getty Images: 9, 17, 32, 39, 41. Jeff Gross/Getty Images: front cover. L. Hammerness/BEI/Rex Features: 22. Frazer Harrison/Getty Images: 35. Harry How/Getty Images: 6, 10c, 12, 13, 21, 31, 33. Zack Podell/Action Plus/Topfoto: 4, 38. Christian Pondella/Getty Images: 2, 8, 15, 20, 24, 25, 26, 30, 34, 36. Sipa Press/Rex Features: 10-11. styley/Rex Features: 16. Alex Sudea/Rex Features: 40. Topfoto; 18. Hector Vivas/Jam Media/Latin Content/Getty Images: 28-29. S.Winner/Shutterstock: 19.

RD/6000006415/001
May 2012

Contents

Words highlighted in the text can be found in the glossary.

Welcome to the X-Games

Shaun White on his way to winning gold in the X-Games Skateboard Vert final in 2011.

The X-Games brings together athletes from around the world. The summer sports competition showcases skateboarding, **BMX**, rally car racing, and **Moto X** competitions. If you're an action sports star, there's no bigger competition than the X-Games.

The X is short for "Extreme," and the games host a range of difficult, exciting—and dangerous events. The Summer X-Games are usually held every year in August, while the Winter X-Games are held in January or February. Competitors compete to win gold, silver, and bronze medals, as well as prize money.

eXtreme fact

The first X-Games were held in the summer of 1995 in Rhode Island and were watched by almost 200,000 people.

Appearances by top competitors, such as Tony Hawk (shown above), attracted huge crowds.

At the X-Games, action sports stars show off their latest tricks. In the 1999 Best Trick competition, skateboarder Tony Hawk landed the world's first "**900.**" That's 2½ spins while airborne! He had failed 11 times already. He was over the time limit. But none of the other skaters protested. They wanted to see him make history.

eXtreme fact

Events at the Summer X-Games change from year to year, depending on what is new and exciting. The very first games included:

- **Bungee jumping**
- **Inline skating**
- **Skysurfing**
- **Sport climbing**

What's the Thrill?

What makes the X-Games so special? Superb athletes strutting their stuff, the stunts, the thrills —and more than anything—the danger!

Action sports stars, such as Travis Pastrana, push themselves to the limit. Here he is competing in the Moto X Speed and Style event.

Like the Olympics, the X-Games are about skill and speed. Crowds flock to the X-Games to watch daredevil skaters and riders in action. These athletes perform death-defying stunts, especially in the high-flying "Big **Air**" skateboarding and Moto X events.

eXtreme fact

During his career, X-Games motorcycle legend Travis Pastrana has had 17 operations on his knees, operations on his shoulder, wrists, and elbow, and more broken bones than he can remember.

Why do action sports stars do it? Many love the thrill of being the first to land an impossible trick. If they pull off a wickedly dangerous stunt without getting injured, it can make them famous.

In 2003, 13-year-old Ryan Sheckler made history when he won the Skateboard Street event, becoming the youngest X-Games gold medalist ever. One of his trademark tricks is the kick-flip indy.

eXtreme fact

X-Games athletes are often very young—like their fans. In 2006, skater Nyjah Huston became the youngest competitor in X-Games history. He came second in the Street finals, when he was just 11 years old!

Nyjah Huston during the 2010 X-Games men's Skateboard Street final.

BMX Ballet

Bicycle Moto X, or BMX, is all about extreme racing, "getting air," and stunts performed on tough bicycles.

BMX racing has been around since the 1970s, when the first heavy-duty bike frames appeared. During the 1980s, riders like Matt Hoffman invented dozens of the pavement and midair, or "aerial" tricks that now feature in the X-Games Street and Vert BMX competitions.

(Right) Daniel Dhers' gold medal performance in the BMX Freestyle Park competition in 2010.

BMX riding has come a long way since the early races on dirt tracks. Here, Jamie Bestwick soars high in the BMX Vert event.

The freestyle BMX bikes used in the X-Games are built to suit individual riders and their style. The tires are designed for the smooth surfaces of pavements and jumps.

eXtreme fact

The freestyle bikes used in the X-Games have a steel frame for strength. The aluminum frames of the BMX racing bikes used in the Olympics make them light and fast.

BMX Street and Park

There are four BMX events at the X-Games. While BMX racing became an Olympic event at the 2008 Beijing Games, the X-Games are home to skillful and daring BMX freestyle events: Street, Park, Vert, and Big Air.

In the Street event, riders perform tricks on a course that includes railings, steps, and other obstacles that might be found on your street. At X-Games 17 in 2011, the course was set out like a real street, including pipes and raised flowerbeds to **grind**.

Ty Morrow jumps a rail on the "real street" Street course at X-Games 17.

The Freestyle Park is the ultimate mashup event. It combines the balancing skills of Street with the airborne skills of the **halfpipe**. In a typical competition, riders are given three rides to perform whatever tricks they want in a set time. They can also use whatever part of the course they want. The judges award points for difficulty, style, variety, and best use of the ramps.

The Freestyle Park playing field includes:

- **Obstacles a rider would find on the street, such as railings.**
- **The vert ramps, slopes, spines, and box jumps of a prebuilt BMX park.**

Brett Banasiewcz performs a front flip in the BMX Freestyle Park final during X-Games 16.

BMX Vert and Big Air

Chad Kagy gets tricky during the X-Games Vert finals.

In the Vert event, riders perform "gravity" tricks in the halfpipe. This is a wooden semicircle roughly 10 feet (3 m) high.

A typical run involves going from one side to the other, flying high above the top of the halfpipe, then landing on the downward slope—or **transition**. Riders also pull off "**lip** tricks" on the **coping** at the top of the ramp.

The riders compete in a **jam** format, taking turns to make their runs.

eXtreme fact

Top BMX pro riders can jump 10 feet (3 m) above the coping—the edge at the top of the halfpipe.

A rider goes hands-free during a flip in the Big Air competition.

BMX Big Air is the most daring of the bike events. Competitors drop in on a ramp 10 stories high and jump over a 60-foot (18-m) gap. They land on a **quarterpipe** that shoots them four stories into the air. Your heart pounds just watching them!

Riders perform tricks while in the air. In the 2009 Summer X-Games, Anthony Napolitan amazed the crowd by landing the world's first double front flip on a bicycle.

eXtreme fact

BMX Big Air is always tough on the athletes. In the 2011 BMX Big Air event, no fewer than seven riders slammed hard onto the Mega Ramp. Even the eventual winner, Steve McCann, went over the handlebars twice while attempting a double front flip.

BMX Superstars

The X-Games have turned many BMX riders into global superstars.

Matt Hoffman

A giant in the world of BMX Freestyle is Matt Hoffman. He is nicknamed "The Condor," thanks to his ability to soar high above the halfpipe. At just 15 years old, he invented a whole new world of vert tricks on the halfpipe. One of his most famous is the "Flip-**Fakie,**" a **backflip** landed backward! In 2002, Hoffman became the first person to successfully execute a "no-handed 900" in competition.

Matt Hoffman is considered by many to be the greatest BMX Vert rider in history.

Garrett Reynolds

Garrett Reynolds is one of the best BMX Freestyle riders around. He began competing at the age of 12, turning **professional** the following year. In 2011, he bagged his ninth X-Games gold medal in Street BMX. Other riders call him the "Park Shark," because he always eats up the competition!

eXtreme fact

By 2009, BMX legend Dave Mirra had won an incredible 24 medals at the X-Games, the highest number in any X-Games sport.

Garrett Reynolds at X-Games 16.

Jamie Bestwick

Almost unbeatable in the last few years, in 2011, British rider Jamie Bestwick made BMX Vert history after winning five golds in a row—known as a five-peat. Incredibly, this high-flying BMX wizard lists his greatest fear as "heights"!

Crazy About Moto X

In Motocross, or Moto X, the best motorcycle riders on the planet gather to perform acrobatic stunts or to race one another.

Cross-country motorcycle racing started in Britain in the 1930s, when it was known as scrambling (above, right). During the 1990s, riders began doing tricks at the end of races, creating the sport of Freestyle Motocross, or Moto X. They learned how to perform incredible aerial stunts, copying tricks from snowboarders and BMX riders.

eXtreme fact

To protect themselves, riders wear:

- Helmets and goggles
- Leather gloves
- Leather boots with steel toe caps
- Body armor under their shirts
  This is a plastic shield lined with a layer of foam
- Neck brace for very dangerous stunts

Moto X riders modify their bikes in many ways. Some cut grips into the seat, so they can hang onto the bike while letting go of the handlebars. Many riders also shorten the width of the handlebars. This makes it easier to swing their legs around the bars in tricks such as the "Heelclicker." A metal pipe or "lever" coming off the handlebars helps a rider keep their balance in midair during stunts such as the "Kiss of Death" backflip.

Super X and Enduro X

Super X, or Supercross, is a thrill a second. Ten motorcycle riders charge around a course packed with crowd-pleasing obstacles such as ramps and dark tunnels.

The Supercross course is built inside a big stadium. Along with huge mounds of hard-packed dirt, there's a big hill to climb, massive wooden ramps, and even a concrete wall. The highly competitive riders shoot out of the gate. A fast start is all-important. The rider who is quickest to the first corner, the "**holeshot,**" often wins the race. In 2011, Super X was run as a women's event—called Moto X Women's Racing.

Ashley Fiolek leaps over a dirt mound during the Super X event at X-Games 16.

The jumps in the Super X course are 42–82 feet (13–25 m) long. They make the riders shoot almost 66 feet (20 m) into the air.

Eric Sorby and Matt Oppen take a tumble on the boulders obstacle during the Enduro X competition.

In 2011, a new Moto X event was born—Enduro X. Here riders battle with dirt, sand, logs, and boulders as well as one another. They get stuck on obstacles and heavy falls are common. For added thrills, organizers add water to the course, making it a real battle to finish at all! Women also took part in Enduro X. Maria Forsberg took gold in her first ever X-Games.

eXtreme fact

Taddy Blazusiak won the first ever Enduro X competition held at X-Games 17. He was so happy he jumped up and down. He said afterward, "I'm really happy, I had a steady start, I wasn't going over my head, and I just worked my way through."

Fabulous Freestyle

Freestyle motorcycle riders perform stunning tricks while jumping distances of 98 feet (30 m) or more. It takes many hours of practice each day to develop a new trick. No wonder many are practiced on a BMX bike first!

Travis Pastrana caught in action during the Freestyle event.

In the early days of Freestyle riding, riders refined and improved simple tricks such as no-handers and no-footers. The stunts became more and more daring. In the "Kiss of Death," the rider does a handstand with their head touching the front mudguard! The 2002 Summer X-Games saw the first backflip.

eXtreme fact

Today's riders perform backflip variations with names like the "Shaolin Flip" and the "Cliffhanger."

The Best Trick event allows riders to showcase their biggest tricks. Riders push themselves hard. In the 2008 Summer X-Games, Jim Dechamp was badly injured when he tried a front flip and crashed.

Moto X Speed and Style combines racing with scores for tricks performed in the first three laps.

In Moto X Best Whip, the fans decide which rider has the most stylish "whip" during a 10-minute session. "Whipping" is the rider's skill at rotating and flipping the rear of the bike in the air.

In the Step Up event, riders speed up a ramp and leap over a bar that gets raised higher each round—up to 30 feet (9 m) high.

Ronnie Renner in the Step Up competition. You can see the camera on his helmet for super action video closeups.

Moto X Megastars

A great Moto X rider needs balance, strength, timing, coordination—and courage!

Travis Pastrana

Travis Pastrana was voted Rider of the Decade in 2010. He won the first four X-Games Freestyle events. Then in the 2006 X-Games he won three gold medals, for Best Trick, Moto X Freestyle, and Rally Car Racing. That year, the crowd went wild when Travis Pastrana became the first rider to land a double backflip in competition! It was so risky, he vowed never to do it again—then used it to win the Freestyle event in 2010.

Travis Pastrana gets Moto X Speed and Style gold in 2010.

eXtreme fact

Every rider has his or her own style. "Cowboy" Kenny Bartram got his nickname after wearing a cowboy hat to freestyle events. He has worked as a stunt rider in movies such as the *Fantastic Four.*

eXtreme fact

Deaf since birth, female star Ashley Fiolek has overcome several obstacles, including broken bones, to win the Women's Moto X in both 2009 and 2010.

Mike Metzger

In his final jump during the 2002 X-Games, Mike Metzger landed the first backflip in Moto X Freestyle, then did it again over the second jump.

Kyle Loza

In 2009, Kyle Loza became the first person to win three Best Trick golds in a row, winning the last two with his "Electric Doom" move.

Ashley Fiolek with her Moto X Racing gold medal at X-Games 16.

Live on Stage

When the X-Games comes to town, it's like a big party!

At the X Factory, happy fans meet the stars face to face and get their autographs.

Music is an important part of the X-Games atmosphere. DJs spin tracks during each athlete's run, and there are dance and music events in the evening after the sports events are over.

The X-Games aren't just about watching the stars in action. Fans can show off their own tricks at the BMX park, mini ramp, or skatepark, or tackle climbing walls and video games. BMX stars give tips on how to tune up bikes properly for street and vert tricks. There are also sportbike and technology demonstrations.

eXtreme fact

Many extreme sports, especially skateboarding, have their own music, clothing, and way of talking. Several X-Games stars have set up their own companies to make boards, gear, and clothing designed for their fans.

An X-Games fan poses with a rocket launcher at the Navy booth during the fan fest at X-Games 17.

Gripping Rally Racing

Rally racing is the fastest event at the X-Games. It's also the most hectic, with cars bumping and crashing into one another and launching themselves off jumps.

Rally racing has been around almost as long as the automobile. Rally drivers test their skills in timed "stages" on routes closed to other traffic, from rough forest tracks, ice, and snow to desert sand. Since 2005, the X-Games have brought these off-road gladiators into a big stadium. Racing side-by-side, the cars kick up dust and rocks as they tear around the dirt track.

eXtreme fact

Travis Pastrana won the first X-Games Rally event in dramatic style, after former World Rally Championship winner Colin McRae rolled his car with just a few turns to go.

Unlike most high-performance racing cars, rally cars are very similar to road cars. They can be driven on normal roads as well as race tracks. Though the X-Games course is short, the cars have to work incredibly hard. There are tight turns, steep uphill and downhill slopes, and a huge jump every driver has to tackle at least once.

eXtreme fact

X-Games rally cars have engines that pump out 500 horsepower. They can hit 60 mph (97 km/h) in just two seconds. They cost nearly $500,000 to build!

X-Games Rally and Rally X

In most X-Games events, it's all about the athlete's skill and concentration. The rally events are also a test for the cars' performance and reliability. You never know what is going to happen!

Kenny Brack and Travis Pastrana compete in Rally Car Racing at Summer X-Games 15.

Rally Car Racing combines the drama of traditional rally driving with the big air stunts and jumps the X-Games are famous for. The winner is the car with the lowest time over the set course. There is plenty of exciting action to watch. Even the best drivers can suddenly spin out of control or flip over.

eXtreme fact

In 2008, Andrew Comrie-Picard front-flipped his car over the 69-foot (21-m) gap jump in a spectacular crash. He and his codriver survived.

Dave Mirra competes in the Rally Car SuperRally Final during X-Games 16.

In X-Games 17, Rally X replaced the SuperRally event of previous years. In Rally X, the cars sprint for just a few short laps around the stadium. Four drivers race wheel-to-wheel on the dirt track.

The driving in Rally X is very aggressive. There is a lot of shoving and pushing. Speed off the starting line is all-important. The car that gets ahead at the first corner can be very hard to pass later on in the race.

eXtreme fact

During the Rally X race, drivers must decide when to take an extra, longer lap known as the "joker lap." It features a "gap" jump.

Stars On Four Wheels

In the rally events, the drivers compete in teams run by car manufacturers. While some are specialist drivers, others are star athletes from other X-Games events.

Moto X kings Travis Pastrana and Brian Deegan, and BMX star Dave Mirra, have all made the switch to driving rally cars from other sports. It is tough competing against top drivers such as Sverre Isachsen, the European Rally X champion, and stunt driver Tanner Foust, who in 2010 won both Rally and SuperRally golds at the X-Games.

Travis Pastrana #199 and Brian Deegan #38 race side-by-side during X-Games 16.

Start of the SuperRally Final during X-Games 16.

eXtreme fact

In the X-Games 17 Rally X event, Travis Pastrana competed using a specially adapted steering wheel because he had a broken leg!

In 2009 and 2010, the rally events were held in the famous LA Coliseum, site of the 1932 and 1984 Olympic Games. But in 2011, the race was held for the first time on a longer course in the streets of downtown Los Angeles, with the cars jumping next to buildings! The 2011 Rally Car Race was won by British driver Liam Doran.

X-Games Skateboarding

For most people, skateboarding is just a great way to have fun. But when top athletes push themselves to the limits to pull off dangerous midair stunts, this action sport really is "extreme."

The skateboarding stars of the X-Games are skilled enough to handle tricks that are much too dangerous for regular skaters to try. They are professionals who skate for a living. It takes a special talent and years of training. In the last 30 years, they have taken the sport from simple "ollies" and aerial grabs, to huge gaps, massive railings, and "hairball" (extreme) tricks off the megaramp.

Sandro Dias competes in Skateboard Vert during Summer X-Games 16.

Most of the skateboards used by X-Games stars today are similar to the slim freestyle boards of the 1980s. They have a curved nose and tail, straight sides, and small wheels. Light and easy to flip, they can be used for street, vert, or park skating.

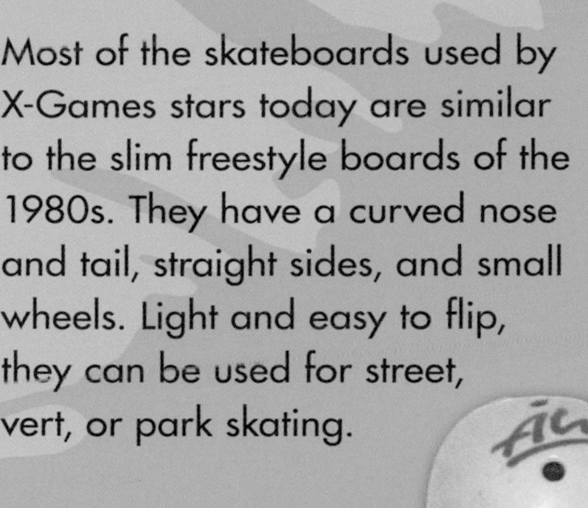

eXtreme fact

Skateboarding pioneer Tony Alva came up with the aerial grab. Another legend, Rodney Mullen, invented dozens of street tricks. He developed the first "kick-flip," where the skater flips the board into the air with his or her toes, then lands on it again.

Nose

Black grip tape (applied to top surface)

Urethane wheels are tough and grip well

Kicktail

Strong trucks to withstand heavy landings

Deck made up of seven layers, or plies, of wood

Park Sharks and Street Style

The Summer X-Games features four skateboarding events: Skateboard Park, Street, Vert, and Big Air.

Curren Caples, age 14, makes a grab at X-Games 16.

Skateboard Park takes place on a fast-flowing course made of concrete and wood. It is built much like a regular skatepark. It has curved sides, called transitions. There are also plenty of spines, box jumps, and rails for skaters to work off.

Skateboard Park is often a clash of new and old styles. Rising stars such as Curren Caples and Pedro Barros challenge veteran pool skaters twice their age!

Skateboard Street takes place in a concrete plaza. Skaters link together tricks performed on obstacles such as stair sets, banks, ledges, boxes, and handrails. Riders are judged on how difficult or original their stunts are, how smoothly their tricks flow together, and how they use the course.

In Skateboard Street, each skater has five runs. Each run lasts 45 seconds—or two crashes!

eXtreme fact

In Real Street, 12 of the top street skaters in the world put forward a 60-second video clip showing their best tricks in action. Fans get to vote for their favorite. Then a panel of expert skaters selects the gold-medal winner.

Skateboarding Vert and Big Air

Vert and Big Air are the two skateboarding events with the biggest wow factor. Over the years, they have featured some of the greatest stars of skateboarding, such as Tony Hawk and Andy Macdonald.

In the Vert competition, skaters pull a variety of spins, flips, and grinds in a U-shaped halfpipe about 60 feet (18 m) wide. This has curved sides that help the skater perform amazing aerial stunts. To go faster and higher, skaters "pump" their boards. They bend their knees as they go into the transition, then stand up as they get near the top.

Vert skaters get good marks for stylish, original, and difficult stunts, and the way they put them together.

Skateboard Big Air is one of the most dangerous events at the X-Games. Riders hurtle down an 82-foot (25-m) "Megaramp." This launches them over a giant 69-foot (21-m) gap. After performing a death-defying mid-air trick, the skaters land in a monster 26-foot- (8-m-) high quarterpipe, where they then try to pull off a breathtaking finishing trick. It is a high-risk event and spectacular falls are common.

eXtreme fact

In 2007, Australian skater Jake "Ironman" Brown was lucky to walk away alive after he lost control of his skateboard and fell four stories onto the ramp. He went on to win the Big Air event in 2009 and 2010.

Female skater Gaby Ponce won her first gold in the 2010 Women's Skateboard Vert.

Vert and Big Air skaters always wear a lot of protective gear:

- **Helmets**
- **Knee and elbow pads**
- **Wrist guards**

Skating Giants

Bob Burnquist competing in 2007.

Ten years ago, few could match the amazing vert skills of skating genius Tony Hawk. Though he no longer competes, the "Birdman" still comes up with cutting-edge tricks to keep younger skaters on their toes!

Andy Macdonald

Skating legend Andy Macdonald, known as the "Mac Attack," holds the record for the most X-Games skateboarding medals—an incredible 21 by 2010. Another veteran star is Brazilian Bob Burnquist, who turned pro at 14. His spectacular run in the 2001 Vert was almost enough to make commentator Tony Hawk lose his voice! He is also the only skater to go over a loop ramp with a gap in it.

eXtreme fact

Bob Burnquist almost killed himself when he missed the rail attempting a 50–50 grind into the Grand Canyon. But he nailed the stunt the second time around.

Rune Glifberg and Pierre-Luc Gagnon

Two other big medal-winners are Danish skater Rune Glifberg and Canadian Pierre-Luc Gagnon. Glifberg is known for his stylish pool riding, while Gagnon was first to **three-peat** in the X-Games Vert competition in 2010.

Lyn-Z Adams Hawkins

Lyn-Z Adams Hawkins is one of the best-known female skaters. By 2010, she had won seven medals, including three golds. She's also a talented surfer and snowboarder.

Lyn-Z Adams Hawkins performs on her way to winning the Silver Medal during the Women's Skateboard Vert final at X-Games 16.

X-Games Asia

X-Games Asia, held in Shanghai, China, allows Summer X-Games stars like Bob Burnquist and Andy Macdonald to show off their skills in front of extreme sports fans in the Far East.

X-Games Asia is a smaller version of the main Summer X-Games, with BMX and Skateboard Vert and Street competitions. In the Big Air event, skaters and BMX riders have to tailor their stunts to suit the Mini MegaRamp, which is smaller than the giant ramp in the Summer X-Games.

Mini MegaRamp is a scaled-down version of the one used in the Summer X-Games.

eXtreme fact

The X-Games are truly international. Smaller events have been organized in countries all over the world, including Brazil, Canada, Japan, Korea, Malaysia, Mexico, Singapore, Spain, Taiwan, the Philippines, and Dubai.

Aggressive Inline Skating is very popular in Asia, so there are both Vert and Street competitions in X-Games Asia. Meanwhile, the X-mini Aggressive Inline Skating Team showcases skaters from Japan, China, and Thailand.

Japanese inline skater Takeshi Yasutoko has won four gold medals in the Aggressive Inline Vert competition.

X-Games Medal Tables

X-Games 17 (2011)	1st	2nd	3rd
BMX			
Freestyle Big Air	Steve McCann	Vince Byron	Chad Kagy
Freestyle Park	Daniel Dhers	Dennis Enerson	Scotty Cranmer
Freestyle Street	Garrett Reynolds	Dennis Enerson	Dakota Roche
Vert	Jamie Bestwick	Steve McCann	Vince Byron
Moto X			
Best Trick	Jackson Strong	Cam Sinclair	Josh Sheehan
Best Whip	Jeremy Stenberg	Todd Potter	Jarryd McNeil
Enduro X (Men's)	Taddy Blazusiak	Mike Brown	Justin Soule
Enduro X (Women's)	Maria Forsberg	Tarah Gieger	Kacy Martinez
Freestyle	Nate Adams	Adam Jones	Dany Torres
Speed and Style	Nate Adams	Mike Mason	Ronnie Faisst
Step Up	Matt Buyten	Ronnie Renner	Myles Richmond
Women's Racing	Vicki Golden	Tarah Gieger	Livia Lancelot
Rally Car Racing	Liam Doran	Marcus Gronholm	David Higgins
Rally Car Rally X	Brian Deegan	Tanner Foust	Marcus Gronholm
Skateboard			
Big Air	Bob Burnquist	Adam Taylor	Edgard Pereira
Park	Raven Tershy	Pedro Barros	Ben Hatchell
Street (Men's)	Nyjah Huston	Luan Oliveira	Ryan Sheckler
Street (Women's)	Marisa Dal Santo	Alexis Sablone	Leticia Bufoni
Vert	Shaun White	Pierre-Luc Gagnon	Bucky Lasek

Web Sites & Glossary

http://espn.go.com/action/xgames/summer/2011
The awesome ESPN gateway to their Summer X-Games coverage, including videos, photo galleries, competitor biographies, interviews, and results, a cellphone app (so you can stay up-to-date with everything happening on the scene), plus podcasts, and Twitter feeds.

http://jamiebestwick.com
Jamie Bestwick's blog, featuring current news, photos, with links to Facebook, Twitter, and the Bestwick Foundation.

http://ashleyfiolek.com
Ashley Fiolek's web site includes her up-to-date biography, links to social media sites, plus photos.

http://www.andymacdonald.com
Check out "Andycam" here on Andy Macdonald's web site. There are also photos, his blog, and the latest details about Andy's activities and competition results.

Air—Short for aerial. Any time an athlete and their equipment leaves the ground and gets airborne.

Backflip—A backward somersault in the air.

BMX—Bicycle motocross.

Box jump—Two ramps on either side of a platform that is roughly 13–20 feet (4–6 m) across. Used in Park and Street events.

Coping—A round lip at the top of a ramp or obstacle. Can be made of concrete or steel or plastic pipes.

Fakie—To skate or ride backward.

Grind—Sliding along the top of an obstacle such as a railing or lip of a ramp.

Halfpipe—The U-shaped pipe used in the skateboard and BMX Vert events.

Holeshot—The first corner on a Moto X racetrack.

Jam—Timed session, may be 10 or 15 minutes long, in which athletes take turns to perform stunts.

Lip—The top of a jump. Also called the takeoff, because it's the part that can be used by an athlete to fly into the air.

Moto X—Off-road motorcycle riding.

Professional—Doing a certain job for money.

Quarterpipe—A single wall of the halfpipe, used in Park courses and in Big Air events.

Spines—Two ramps placed back-to-back with a small platform on top.

Three-peat—Winning an event three times in a row. A four-peat is four wins in a row and so on.

Transition—The curved sides of a skateboard park course.

Vert—Short for vertical obstacle that slopes straight up into the air, like a pool wall.

Index